CALLED TO MARRIAGE

Journeying Together Toward God

CAROL LUEBERING

ST. ANTHONY MESSENGER PRESS

Cincinnati, Ohio

Nihil Obstat: Rev. Robert L. Hagedorn
Rev. Donald Miller, O.F.M.

Imprimi Potest: Rev. Fred Link, O.F.M.
Provincial

Imprimatur: + Most Rev. Carl K. Moeddel
Vicar General and Auxiliary Bishop
Archdiocese of Cincinnati
January 29, 2001

Scripture citations are taken from the *New Revised Standard Version of the Bible*, copyright ©1989 by the Division of Christian Education of the National Council of Churches of Christ in the U.S.A. Used by permission. All rights reserved.

Front cover photo by Antony Nagelmann/
FPG International LLC, copyright ©1996
Cover design by Mary Alfieri
Book design by Sandy L. Digman
Electronic pagination and format by Sandy L. Digman

ISBN 0-86716-389-5

Published by St. Anthony Messenger Press
www.AmericanCatholic.org

Printed in the U.S.A.

To Jack:

You know how much I hate to travel without a firm itinerary, but this has been quite a trip. I can't imagine having taken this journey with anyone else—thank you.

I love you.

Contents

Journeying Together

O ne June morning back in 1956, Jack Luebering and I
stood in church before our gathered family and
friends. In their presence, we promised to love each
other "until death do us part." Little did we know what
we were doing! We thought we had reached the end of a
journey. We had each found someone with whom we
wanted to spend a lifetime; we were ready to settle into
our vocation as a married couple.

We had always assumed we were called to marriage.
It was, after all, a vocation—even though the priests and
nuns of our generation urged us to listen for a "higher"
calling. Even today, Vocation Sunday homilies often
include marriage almost as an afterthought. (Only the
single life gets less notice.) Yet marriage seems to hold
high favor in the view of God, who calls most people to
travel through life side by side with a husband or a wife.

What we didn't realize on our wedding day is that
marriage is not just something God calls us to at one
point in our lives. Rather, it is also the way God speaks
to us, the way we come to know the One whose
whispered "This one!" set us on this road. The journey
itself is the reechoing call, the way we discover who
God is, how God is with us and for us. What we learn

from the struggle to be faithful in good times and bad slowly carries us deeper and deeper into the divine heart.

The journey is not always easy. We face daily the struggle to balance the budget and our schedules, to deal wisely and lovingly with each other and with other family members. The road we travel is under construction, and we keep hitting detours.

Some of them are as predictable as the construction zones marked on a travel map: adjusting to married life; adjusting—again—to the arrival of children and, years later, their departure; facing retirement and old age together. We expect such events to make changes in our lives. Others strike as suddenly as a blown tire or a traffic jam: a serious illness, a job transfer, a financial setback.

Through all of the crises we encounter, we keep running into the same all-too-familiar orange barrels along our route:

- We stumble over the differences between us.

- We learn that giving life is more than a matter of birth.

- We seek reconciliation for injuries large and small.

- We find our way blocked by pain and sorrow.

- We learn to let go of much—even, finally, of life itself.

And in the difficulties as well as in the joys, we discover what it means to say that God journeys with us. Through them all, we learn more and more about the

nature of the One who awaits us at the journey's end—
the One who *is* the journey's end.

This book is an invitation to look back over the
route you and your spouse have covered so far and to
discern how it has carried you toward God. In each
chapter, you will meet a biblical couple facing one of
these crises. You will see how Scripture tells their story,
and be invited to imagine their feelings and their
struggle.

Contemporary couples will chime in with their
variations on the themes as we explore with the help of
other Scripture texts what we learn about God during
the detours. Finally, you will be asked to look back,
alone or with your spouse, over your own journey and
see how these events have shaped your own understanding of
God.

This is not a how-to book; it will not help you to
resolve a quarrel with your spouse or loosen your grip
on a growing-up child. Neither will it offer a road map
to newlyweds or help repair a failing marriage. Some of
your companions in this volume may, to be sure, tell
you how they made it through the orange barrels. But
the primary invitation in these pages is to reflect on
what God has already written across the map of your
own married life.

LOOKING BACK AT YOUR JOURNEY

* *Look back at the list of "orange barrels" on page 2. How
many of them can you easily recall hitting on your own
marital journey?*

- *How did hitting these obstacles affect your concept of God?*

- *Name as many things as you can that you have learned about God and God's ways from journeying with your spouse.*

CHAPTER ONE

Falling for Each Other

OUR CALL FROM A LOVING GOD

And the rib that the LORD God had taken from the man he made into a woman and brought her to the man.

Then the man said,
  "This at last is bone of my bones
    and flesh of my flesh...."—GENESIS 2:22-23

I magine Adam gasping in wonder at the creature who stands before him. Unlike all the other forms of life that populate the garden, this one is of his own kind. He has given all the animals names, but only this being can speak his own—and pronounce it with a beguiling smile. Here at last is someone who can ease the inexplicable loneliness that has haunted him. She is like him, yes—but at the same time breathtakingly different. He can't take his eyes off that body! Something he has never felt before stirs within him as he reaches out to touch her.

Eve, too, responds with delight. Before God clothed the man's rib with flesh, it lay near his beating heart.

When Adam clasps the newly formed woman in his arms, Eve once again feels his heart throbbing against her, and she is home.

This couple, gasping at each other's naked beauty, will use their bodies, as we do, to establish ties: to touch, smile and speak, to make love and to share a meal. They will laugh and weep, sigh and shrug. And with these bodily signs, they will open the depths of their hearts to each other. Together in love they will make one whole, one God-breathed body.

Hearing the Call

Adam and Eve fell in love at first sight. The divine Matchmaker's call reached them directly and immediately—but, of course, each of them faced only one potential lover. They did not have to sort through a field of potential mates, as we did. To us, God's call to travel through life together comes much less directly.

Our first parents entered into an arranged marriage. Throughout history, most couples have expected love to follow the wedding in marriages their families arranged—a pattern that still holds in many cultures today. To our surprise, most people do find love in such marriages. Perhaps that is because God's dream that man and woman will cling to each other and become one flesh is written deep in the human heart. Or perhaps it is because the couple in an arranged marriage have some important things in common: They come from the same culture and share similar family backgrounds. More importantly, they share the expectation that love comes after the wedding.

Our cultural expectations are very different. We expect to fall in love first and then to marry. Further, we assume that love matters enough to bridge even wide disparities in two people's backgrounds.

And sometimes it does. My mother's family tree contains couples whose love overcame not only cultural differences but even downright enmity. My English Lutheran grandmother married an Irish Catholic over her parents' objections. One of my great-grandmother's English ancestors eloped with a bewitching Dutch girl in New York when the two groups were still deeply at odds; the bride's father forbade her ever to return home. Not only were the English and Dutch squabbling over possession of New York (or New Amsterdam, take your pick), they didn't even speak the same language. My dad, who came from solidly German stock, prepared his family's traditional Christmas sausage for his new in-laws with great misgivings about its reception.

My friend Maureen, who comes from Irish stock, knew her family would have a problem when she fell in love with the son of Japanese immigrants. What surprised her was that his family wasn't crazy about a marriage, either.

Love conquers all, the old saying goes. Sometimes it does—but never easily. God calls us to help it triumph.

Falling in Love

Sometimes love seems to begin, as it did for Adam and Eve, in the space of a heartbeat. Two strangers meet and are instantly and powerfully drawn to each other. It happened that way for Sandy back in the 1920's. He was a campus hero who held letters in three sports, served as a class officer and somehow found time to make excellent grades. A 'sheik' in the parlance of his day, he was a handsome fellow who could often be found surrounded by a bevy of flirtatious females.

One day, a pretty young woman walked by such a gathering with her friends. "Look, there's Sandy!" one whispered. "Let's go talk to him."

As her friends rushed to join the admiring circle, Liddie tossed back her long black hair and walked on. Sandy looked after her. "Who is that?" he asked—and soon found his way to her door. For nearly fifty years, my dad answered his own question by calling her his wife.

More often, love develops gradually over a period of time. Two strangers meet and slowly discover how much they have in common. Shared tastes and views and interests draw them into friendship, and friendship slowly ripens into a burning desire to spend their lives together.

Tim and Kay, for example, met in a medical setting. As a college student he suffered a badly injured leg in an accident. She was the therapist who patiently saw him through to full recovery. When they began to meet socially as well as professionally, they didn't even call it dating at first. They were just good friends for several years.

It wasn't until Tim was considering a job offer in a distant state that they suddenly realized they didn't want to be apart. Soon there was an engagement ring on Kay's finger. When they announced the news to their families and friends, they were astounded to discover that the love that had caught them both off guard came as no surprise at all to anyone else.

Whether it hits us like a thunderbolt or slowly creeps up on us, we rightfully speak of *falling* in love. Taking a tumble is an unsettling experience. We lose our balance and with it our sense of control. Our certainty about the immediate future hangs suspended until we can pick ourselves up and check for damage.

And so it is when we fall in love. The world whirls giddily in orbit around a brand-new sun, setting many a previous certainty spinning off into space. Strange things happen to time: It whizzes past when we are together with our loved one and creeps when we are apart. We toss our plans for the future back on the drawing board, and we view everything through a pleasant rosy glow.

Rethinking God

Any event, whether joyous or tragic, that shifts the moorings of our personal worlds calls our concepts of God into question. When life goes terribly awry, we may wonder if God isn't a bully—or at least uncaring. When life is sweet, we think of God as a generous giver who scatters blessings liberally.

From our early religious training and from the pages of Scripture, we glean many images. Often they are contradictory. God is the architect of creation whose works leave us gasping in wonder at the brim of the Grand Canyon and the wrathful being who will one day destroy the world we know. God is the judge to whom we must all one day answer for our failings and the tender shepherd who seeks each lost lamb. God rewards the faithful with success in this world and is the champion of the poor and oppressed. God is the liberator who leads people to freedom and the lawgiver who places limits on our freedom.

Discovering a love meant to last is a blinding revelation of the God who is Lover, the God who takes a people as his bride. As someone once put it, "There is no surprise as magical as the surprise of being loved. It is God's finger on one's shoulder." And so it is. Being touched by love is an encounter with the God who *is* Love.

Looking back over thirty years of marriage, Judy recalls a Sunday when she was still a newlywed: "The second reading was from 1 John 4. 'God is love,' it said; 'and those who abide in love abide in God, and God abides in them.' It was one of those 'Aha! moments,'" she says, "the first time God became really real to me. I had never thought of God that way before, yet suddenly I could name the sense of being part of something larger than myself that falling in love had given me."

The experience is powerful and enduring. When my mother-in-law lay dying, she confessed her concern for her husband of fifty-five years. He thought *he* took care of *her*. He made the big decisions for both of them— where they would live, when they needed a new car, how to invest their savings. But she knew well how helpless he was when it came to the details of everyday life. He had never even fixed his own breakfast until she was terminally ill. He had no idea how to use the washing machine or the vacuum cleaner. She couldn't imagine how he could live alone.

I tried to reassure her. "Don't worry, Mom," I said.

"He can live with us if he needs to."

She just shook her head. "He's not always easy to live with. And you have never been in love with him."

Learning How God Loves

But falling in love, as life has taught us, is only the beginning. It takes the rest of our married lives to figure out what it really means to love someone. That, indeed, is our call from the God whose Son commanded us to love one another: to explore the meaning of love in our living together. In that way, we catch our clearest glimpse on earth of the God whose love brought us into being and sustains us throughout our lives.

What is this thing called love? Songwriters and poets, dramatists and lovers themselves have long wrestled with that question. Part of it is, of course, the miracle that left Adam breathless: the marvelous chemistry of physical attraction. The intense desire to join one's body to a beloved other's is a powerful binding force. The intimacy we share in bed nourishes and enriches our love for each other. It spills over into every aspect of our lives together with our spouses.

But all too often, chemistry alone fails to last, and couples once strongly drawn to each other drift apart. For truly satisfactory sexual union is more than physical. Because we are creatures of spirit as well as flesh, our lovemaking not only gives great pleasure, it also expresses love, dispels loneliness and enables us to speak with our whole selves when joy seeks celebration or sorrow cries out for comfort.

So there's more to it than sex. We human beings

seldom marry the first person who rings our bells in that way. Neither does promising lifelong fidelity turn the physical attraction switch permanently off. "When I quit looking," grins long-married George, "they'll be patting my face with a shovel."

But neither does that fine first rapture of really falling in love last. We settle into everyday comfort with each other.

Elizabeth remembers a day several years into their marriage when she asked John, "Why do you love me?"

"Because I'm used to you," he replied.

His answer infuriated her. "I was looking for romance," she says. "I expected the sort of thing he'd say when we were courting: 'Because you're beautiful, because you have such a sparkling sense of humor, because you light up the grayest sky for me.' All I got was the sort of thing he might say about his ratty old sneakers.

"Then I got to thinking about the beginning of our marriage, when getting used to each other took a lot of work. Now we can read each other's moods and needs pretty well; then it was no snap. And I realize that I love him because I'm used to him, too. And when I realized that I love being used to him, I fell in love with him all over again."

The Reechoing Call

We continue to fall in love again and again throughout our years together, for God's call is a persistent bidding, not a once-and-for-all invitation. The magical surprise of love continues to catch us off guard;

we fall time and time again. Any number of things can trigger a fresh tumble.

It was another wondrous experience, the arrival of their first child, that sent Laurie and David falling head over heels again. "I watched her nursing Tammy," David says, "and I thought my wife was the most beautiful creature I had ever seen. She made me think of all those beautiful Madonnas the Old Masters painted. I understood for the first time why the sight of a nursing mother inspired them to create such works."

"David never showed much interest in babies," Laurie adds. "He was good with little kids, but he used to say that babies all looked alike to him. But when she was only minutes old, Tammy curled her little hand around his finger and around his heart. I watched him fall in love with her and I fell hard for both of them."

Great joys are not the only events that make our hearts skip a beat. It was a brush with death that stirred the flames in Katie's heart. "Bill had non-Hodgkin's lymphoma," she explains. "The doctor was blunt about his chances—slim. The treatments were rough, and nothing worked. His disease progressed until his only chance was a bone marrow transplant. They had to destroy his own marrow first, and the therapy nearly killed him. It really would have killed him had the transplant failed. I'll never forget how he looked lying in that hospital bed. But it worked! And I don't think I can ever take him for granted again."

"Me either," Bill adds. "I was scared and depressed. There just wasn't any fight left in me. But I'd look at Katie and think, 'I don't want to leave this woman.' I clung to her for dear life—and dear life it is!"

Choosing to Fall

Life-shattering events, whether happy or painful, are certainly part of God's call to us. Maybe God sits up in heaven and decides to send joy or sorrow into a person's life, as many folks think. More likely, such events are just part of the confused world we inhabit. In any case, they shake the ground we once thought solid. We have to pick ourselves up and start over again; they make us rethink the course of our lives and our relationship with God.

In any case, major upsets are pretty rare. Mostly we settle so comfortably into the all-too-predictable that we forget how magical love is. Rather than being consumed by a grand passion, we fall into the habit of expressing love by making such unromantic gestures as cleaning the ring out of the bathtub or depositing a paycheck in the joint account. And sometimes love stays alive only because we work at recovering the magic.

"I was ready to walk," Anne admits. "Gary was under a lot of pressure at work, and was investing all his energy in his job. My job is demanding, too—but everything having to do with running a household and raising two kids was falling on my shoulders. My complaints went unanswered. 'This project won't last forever,' he'd say. It sure seemed like forever!

"I found myself wondering why I ever married him. Then one night when he was working late, I decided to sit down and figure out why. I remembered the fellow I fell in love with, how I admired his ambition and stick-to-itiveness—the very qualities that were causing our present difficulties. I realized that his focus on tomorrow had always given him a kind of freedom from worrying about the details of daily life. He always could deal with chaos at home better than I could. And now I was killing myself to meet my own expectations, not his.

"I also remembered that we were strapped for time together even when we were newlyweds. He was finishing his degree, and we were both working. We had no long, lovely evenings together; we just stole moments for a quick backrub or a bowl of ice cream.

"'We can do that again,' I thought. I'd rather have a few sweet minutes with him than a lifetime without him. And sweet minutes are what I've been trying to schedule in ever since."

In the long run, love isn't just something we feel. Love is something we decide to do. Otherwise, how could Jesus even suggest that loving an enemy is possible? When he told the story of the Good Samaritan (Luke 10:30-35), his listeners surely gaped with horror. Centuries of racial and religious hatred lay between Israel and Samaria. The Good Samaritan chose to lay aside his feelings to tend the wounded man's needs. And he wrote a blank check when he promised to reimburse the innkeeper for any additional expenses.

We signed a blank check on our wedding day. We promised to be faithful and loving in good times and bad, in wealth and poverty, in health and sickness. And we made the check good just as the Good Samaritan did: by tending each other's needs—physical and emotional, day in and day out—regardless of the moment's feelings.

Discovering that we can act lovingly regardless of our feelings has a curious effect on our hearts, for our feelings can follow our actions as easily as they can inspire them. Love becomes a habit that is harder and harder to break as the years roll by. Slowly we begin to understand why God continues to love us: not because we are always such wonderful people, but because the divine heart has grown used to us—and loves being used to us.

LOOKING BACK AT YOUR JOURNEY

- *Recall your first meeting. What first impression did the person you later married make on you? What first attracted you to this person?*

- *When did you realize that you were seriously in love? How did it feel to discover that your partner felt the same way?*

- *When do you remember falling in love all over again with your husband or wife?*

- *How has the experience of falling in love been the magical touch of God's finger on your shoulder? What insights has working at love given you into the nature of God?*

- *How has loving your spouse led you to the God who is Love?*

CHAPTER TWO

Celebrating the Differences

OUR CALL FROM AN ALL-EMBRACING GOD

*Now the LORD said to Abram, "Go from your
country and your kindred and your father's house to
the land that I will show you. I will make of you a
great nation...."*

*So Abram went, as the LORD had told him; and Lot
went with him.... Abram took his wife Sarai and his
brother's son Lot, and all the possessions that they
had gathered, and the persons whom they had
acquired in Haran; and they set forth to go to the
land of Canaan.*—GENESIS 12:1-2, 4-5

The journey Abraham and Sarah set out on four
millennia ago was long and arduous. They trekked
from Ur across many miles of hot and dusty country
to distant Canaan, where they knew no one. It also led
them deep into the heart of God and into the pages of
our history. With the Jews and Muslims, we still revere
them as our ancestors in faith.

Abraham chose to trust the voice he heard. Sarah
heard no voice; she had no choice but to trust her

husband. To her surely fell the practical details of packing up a large household and all its goods, the painful task of saying good-bye to friends and neighbors without being able to explain exactly why. Not only were wives in their society expected to oversee such mundane details while their husbands turned their attention to more important matters, Sarah was better equipped for the role. Reading through the many chapters of Genesis (12—25) that tell their story shows that Sarah had a much more practical bent than Abraham.

He was the visionary who heard God's voice. Abraham believed the incredible promise of a son born of aging Sarah; he was willing to set out in blind trust on a journey to the land of promise. He was what you might call a step-one, step-ten man. Step one: Pick up and go—where? Why? Step ten: Give birth to a great nation—how? He even obeyed without question the command to take Isaac, the long-promised son, to Moriah and offer him in sacrifice. (Don't you wonder what he said to Sarah when he set out and when he returned—or what that long-married woman sensed in his demeanor?)

To Sarah, Abraham must have seemed a dreamer who always had his head at least partway in the clouds. Certainly he was a good provider; back home he held good lands and healthy flocks. All the couple lacked was children—a perpetual heartache. But Abraham thought he could solve that problem by trekking off across the desert!

When they passed through Egypt along the way, he claimed Sarah was his sister, lest some mighty Egyptian kill him to acquire the woman who was so beautiful in his eyes. Sarah must have loved that solution: She ended up in the house of Pharaoh himself! How could Abraham have known that God would afflict the king until he sent them both packing, enriched by the livestock and slaves Pharaoh had paid for Sarah?

When they settled in their new home, Sarah tired of hearing about the promised son her old body was to produce. The practical woman took matters into her own hands and sent her maidservant, Hagar, to Abraham's bed. She later regretted that decision when Hagar flaunted her swelling belly; this problem Sarah solved by driving her rival away into the desert. And when some passing strangers promised Abraham a son by Sarah within the year, she sat behind the tent flap with her apron over her face, trying to stifle her giggles. (She named the boy Isaac, which means "laughter.")

Yes, it was a long and difficult journey they took. Perhaps it was longer for Sarah, though she closed her eyes in death long before her husband. For she had to go far to reach the point where he started out: faith in a God wholly unlike the gods of their native land.

The Attraction of Opposites

Sarah and Abraham were in some respects as different as two people can be. That is probably true of most married couples.

Certainly our likenesses draw us together. Two people in love speak glowingly of what they have in common—right down to a shared passion for football or a like distaste for vegetables. More important are the deeply held values and attitudes they discover in each other. As one starry-eyed bride puts it, "It's as if we were born with the same melody running through our heads."

But husband and wife must learn to become one by singing not in unison but in blending two very different voices in harmony. For we fall in love first of all because someone is not like us physically. (Remember Adam gasping at shapely Eve.) Neither is the other the same in less tangible ways.

There is some truth in the old adage that opposites attract. The differences certainly appealed to a shy young woman named Anne Morrow and the dashing aviator Charles Lindbergh, to the bold, handsome poet Robert Browning and the delicate invalid Elizabeth Barrett. Startling disparity adds the spice of mystery to an unfolding relationship for many people. We don't, after all, fall in love with the image we see in the mirror—at least, not outside of Greek mythology, where the good-looking Narcissus became fatally enamored of his own reflection in a pool.

Actually, it would be pretty boring to live with someone who is exactly like us. What enchanting surprises would we hold for each other?

Sometimes the very differences that draw us together put us off at first. One summer nearly half a century ago, I wrote my college roommate that my three-month stay with my sister held little promise of romance. The only eligible male on the scene was the son of the neighbors who lived behind her, "a boring engineer type."

We met over the back fence. He grew very

conscientious about going out to burn the trash. (Those were the bad old days, ecologically speaking.) My two-year-old nephew spent so much time on the swing he is probably still dizzy in his middle age. By summer's end, things had become very serious; by Christmas, we were engaged. And the neighbors gave us a wire trash burner as a shower gift.

Certainly we choose our friends for the things we have in common. But perhaps we fall in love because the other person is also *unlike* us, because we sense that person has something important that is lacking in our own makeup. Some personality factor we lack—even one we have suppressed—holds out a promise of completion.

The ancient Greek philosopher Plato once proposed that man and woman were one entity until the gods, angered at some misdeed, separated them. Ever since, he said, the two seek the lost half of themselves. Just so, in the person we choose to marry we find someone who is, as the design on one couple's wedding program proclaimed, "the other half of my soul."

The differences between husband and wife hold a promise of completion beyond the marriage bed. As a couple, they can be what neither can be alone: both outgoing and reflective, both practical and imaginative, both organized and spontaneous, both masculine and feminine. This one at last, all lovers say with Adam and Eve, is indeed bone of my bone and flesh of my flesh; this one is the other half of myself.

The Hidden Snag

Ah, but there's a catch. The very differences that capture our hearts raise barriers to understanding each other.

The Genesis story gives no credence to a popular author's theory that men are from Mars and women from Venus. Both originated on the planet Earth, shaped by divine hands and breathed into life by God's love.

The Creator must have a fancy for variety, for the earth teems with life forms. Plants range from single-celled organisms to giant sequoias. The animal world boasts creatures that can soar through the skies and blind, legless animals that live in perpetual darkness deep below the ground. Even the insect population embraces some 750,000 known species, of which most humans can name only a few.

Only one species of the animal we call human walks the earth. There are some six billion of us, and the number continues to escalate. We vary in race and color and language. No two of us are exactly alike; not even genetically identical twins share the same personality.

The very differences that first draw any two of us together also separate us—beginning with the appealing fact that we come in two genders. "The trouble is not that we're from different planets," one woman explains. "The problem is that he speaks Greek and I speak Chinese."

That's more than a difference in vocabulary. Greek is a language of clarity. The tenses of its verbs are clear from their form, as is the purpose a noun serves in a sentence. Using an alphabet borrowed from the Phoenicians, its written form corresponds to the sound of the spoken words. It quite naturally gave rise to the logical thought patterns that were ancient Greece's gift to the Western world.

Chinese, on the other hand, is a language filled with ambiguity. One must listen not only to the spoken word but also to its tone, for a change in pitch sometimes radically alters a word's meaning. (Think, for example, how shifting the accent in the English word *invalid* can make "an ailing person" "null and void.")

The ancient written form of Chinese expresses concepts in pictographs, stylized drawings. The pictograph symbol meaning house, for instance, becomes peace when the sign for a woman is placed under the roof. Add a second woman—a mother-in-law, perhaps—and domestic warmth flees the page, leaving *quarrel* in its place. One must read the relationships to grasp the word's meaning.

In our culture, whether by nature or by nurture, women listen more closely than men to how something is said. And the men among us prize logical thought, while women by and large focus more on relationships. This is no trivial distinction; it affects even the way we choose between right and wrong. Lawrence Kohlberg's pioneering study of moral development in children tracks growth from rule-keeping to a well-developed sense of justice. His subjects were male. A similar study of women and girls by Carol Gilligan indicates that women are more typically concerned with commitment and compassion.

"Why can't a woman be more like a man?" Henry Higgins sang in *My Fair Lady*. And his question (or its reverse) echoes through every couple's life.

Personality differences add more verses to the discordant song: Why can't one see the possibilities; why can't the other see the problems? Why can't one ever plan ahead; why can't the other let go and enjoy? Why can't one express feelings; why can't the other sense them? And the very differences that once were delightful surprises become friction points in a couple's relationship. The partners may even set out to change each other, to reshape the unique creation that is God's precious gift to each of them—an effort that is inevitably doomed to failure.

Looking back on 45 years of marriage, I have to admit that I still don't understand my husband. Oh, I know him really well after all these years. I know what he likes and what he hates. I can tell you how he will react in any given situation. I know exactly how he ticks—but I will never understand why he ticks that way! And he will say the same of me.

Understanding each other is nice, but it's not at all necessary. The commitment we make on our wedding day is not to understand but to achieve unity, to make from two scraps of breath-infused clay one whole self, one enduring unity. And it surely takes the lifetime we pledge to each other! But it can be done.

Learning to Live Together

The first task we faced as newlyweds was learning to live with the disparities. The beginning of a marriage is a time of discovery, to our dismay as often as to our delight.

Variations in taste and opinions can be worked out

or simply tolerated. After all these years of living with a sports fan, I still have no interest in anything that involves a ball. Jack still thinks opera would be great if they just didn't sing. We decided that there was hope for our future early on in our marriage when the televised football game and the radio broadcast of the Metropolitan Opera played at the same volume—and each of us could tune out the other's choice.

But when it comes to deep-down differences, even the smallest can rankle. Even after retirement, Charlie and Liz will never move at the same pace. "I guess I'm your basic Type A personality," she observes. "I have to keep moving. If I have ten minutes before I have to leave for an appointment, I try to think what I can get done in that time.

"Charlie, on the other hand, can spend hours doing nothing! He can put the simplest thing off forever. I really do try not to nag, but he drives me nuts. After ten years of retirement, is he still relaxing from his high-pressure job? I repeat: He drives me nuts!"

"*I* drive *her* nuts?" Charlie responds. "She always wants everything done right now. The world won't end if I don't change the furnace filters the minute she thinks of it, or if we're not the first ones to arrive at a party. Nothing short of a dire emergency can't wait till I get to it."

"Yeah," Liz retorts. "Once when we were on vacation, the fire alarm in our hotel went off. I'd have hit the stairs with my coat over my nightgown. He had to put his clothes on and get all his stuff back in his pockets— at a snail's pace, of course. I have yet to see that dire emergency.

"But I've had to accept the fact that he can only move in low gear. I try to give him a 15-minute warning before we have to leave and to wait at least a day or two before I ask, 'Did you...?'"

A friend's remark moved Joan from acceptance to appreciation. "He's a morning person," she moans. "He opens his eyes, puts his feet on the floor and is wide-awake. I'm the opposite. I hit my stride in the afternoon and can keep going till the wee hours. But I hate mornings! That made for a hard adjustment when we first lived together. He wanted to talk while the coffee was still brewing. He'd ask questions that required an intelligent answer—'Can we take the car in for a lube job Thursday?'—before I could even think when Thursday was, much less what I was going to do then.

"In time, he learned to read the paper while I drank enough coffee to jump-start my engine, and I thought we had it licked. But when a friend said she and her husband were both night people, I was green with envy. 'How wonderful!' I exclaimed.

"'No it's not,' she answered. 'Neither of us hears the alarm.' And suddenly I was grateful that I never have to. What a gift from God that friend was!"

Steve and Susan reached accommodation with much more difficulty. When the first election day of their marriage rolled around, the conservative Republican remembers, "I was shocked to find out how liberal Susan is. We never discussed politics as such when we were dating, but we did discover we shared a lot of concerns about values in our society. Neither of us thinks poverty should be tolerated in our country; we'd both like to see family values supported."

"All we disagree about is how to reach the goals," laughs Susan. "I don't think we'll ever see eye to eye about the role of government. But we don't fight anymore. We just marvel that we can see such different paths to the same ends."

Taking Delight in the Differences

The God who delights in creation's variety, who dearly loves people of every sort, slowly leads us to see each other from the divine point of view. Over the years, we gradually move from toleration to appreciation until we reach the point where we can actually take delight in our differences from each other.

"I'm an engineer," Tim reports. "It's my job to spot where problems are going to arise from a design. Teresa is quite artistic. She has a real gift for seeing how colors and textures will work together, and is always coming up with ways to improve the house or yard. I can't help pointing out what's wrong with her plan. She used to get really mad at me for being a wet blanket. And I'd accuse her of being impractical.

"We passed our silver anniversary that way. Then one day one of us—I don't remember who—came up with an alternate plan for something she'd suggested and I'd shot down. Suddenly we were a team working together to make a workable version that satisfied both of us—and we've been pooling our gifts ever since.

"If we were all alike, I guess," he muses, "there wouldn't be any need for any of us."

Saint Paul once said much the same thing. Writing to a community rent by division, he described them as the many parts of one body, the Body of Christ.

> *If the whole body were an eye, where would the*
> *hearing be? If the whole body were hearing, where*
> *would the sense of smell be? ... As it is, there are*
> *many members, yet one body. The eye cannot say to*
> *the hand, "I have no need of you," nor again the*
> *head to the feet, "I have no need of you."*
> (1 Corinthians 12:17, 21)

The same is true of the one body a married couple makes in their lovemaking. They need to be different enough to complete each other—and not only in a physical way.

Gina learned this lesson the hard way. She is a responsible person who takes life very seriously. For 23 years, she lived with a husband who was the biggest kid on the block. Bob always had the best joke, the best toys, the best time. Several years after his death, she married a second time—to another guy who is the biggest kid on the block. "I think I made Bob's life miserable," she admits. "I didn't realize until he was gone how important his love of fun was to me. This marriage is going to be happier. This time I'm going to enjoy living with someone who thinks life is all a game—even if I never understand him. And he thinks I'm right for him because, as he puts it, champagne needs a glass, not more bubbles."

Long ago I came across a two-part definition of love that remains my favorite. The first part is the willingness to affirm the other, to take delight in who that person is. The second is the willingness to suffer with or for the other person.

Jesus certainly endorsed the second part. There is no greater love, he said, than to lay down our life for someone (see John 15:13). Yet, over the years, that part has come to look easy. I can't help but suffer with Jack; what hurts him hurts me. And I don't think I'd hesitate to give my life for him.

It's the first part most of us have trouble with on a day-in, day-out basis. When we are at cross-purposes because we are such different people, I try to remember that I married Jack exactly because who he is delighted me. I think of God looking over a brand-new world in the beginning of the Bible and rejoicing that it was good, very good. I guess that's why God made each of us the way we are—for the sheer delight of each of us.

LOOKING BACK AT YOUR JOURNEY

- *What differences help you to complete each other?*

- *How have they caused conflict between the two of you?*

- *In what ways have you learned to celebrate the differences between you?*

- *How has celebrating the differences between you and your spouse made you more tolerant of other people's quirks?*

- *What about your spouse do you think delights God? What about yourself?*

- *What do you suppose God finds delightful in the person whom you find hardest to take?*

- *How has celebrating the differences between you and your spouse led you to the all-embracing God?*

CHAPTER THREE

Giving Life

OUR CALL FROM THE SOURCE

So [the shepherds] went with haste and found Mary
and Joseph, and the child lying in the manger. When
they saw this, they made known what had been told
them about this child; and all who heard it were
amazed at what the shepherds told them. But Mary
treasured all these words and pondered them in her
heart. —LUKE 2:16-19

Mary was surely not the only one who pondered.
Joseph's brain cells must have been firing rapidly,
too. This couple had come to parenthood in a way
so extraordinary as to require much reflection over the
years.

Only Mary had any physical part in Jesus' birth.
Joseph was an adoptive father, welcoming a child who
was not his into his heart and his home. Yet his consent
was just as essential to this infant's birth as Mary's faith-
filled, "Let it be." Without it, mother and unborn child
might both have perished as Joseph himself feared—
under a hail of stones, the penalty for adultery.

Even had they escaped that fate, their survival was iffy, for their society made no provision for the support of an unwed woman and her child.

The Gift of Life

We who marry in the presence of the Source of Life expect to hand on the gift. We only wonder how many babies we will have and when. The marriage rite itself assumes that we will bear children. Again and again its prayers and blessings refer to offspring. Before a bride and groom profess their vows, they are asked if they will accept children from God. Only rarely is that question omitted: It was not put to my widowed father-in-law when he married a second time—but then, bride and groom were both in their eighties.

At any age, love is by its very nature life-giving. Dad's step acquired a new spring. My new mother-in-law snuggled next to him at family gatherings with as bright a glow in her eyes as ever graced a bride a quarter of her age. The love they shared gave each of them new life. Just so, the love you and I share with our spouses is life-giving in countless ways.

From the beginning, our love gave birth to a new being: *You and I* became *we.* That "we" is our first child; we nurture it in the total self-giving of the marriage bed and in the casual touch of a hand as we wait for a pot to boil. We tend its needs day in and day out with tenderness and practical concern, with quiet conversation and mended quarrels. Our call to marriage is always a call to give life, even if we remain childless.

An Essential Element

Love is as essential to life as air and water and food. Without it, old folks wither away in nursing homes at the end of life and newborns fail to thrive at its beginning.

Pat and Jerry adopted an infant son from a Korean orphanage many years ago. Thanks to him, they are now great-grandparents, but it almost didn't turn out that way. The result of a passing liaison between a Korean woman and an American GI, he was, like many other mixed-race babies, not welcome among his mother's people when the war ended. Neither was she. Unable to provide for herself and her baby, the desperate young woman left her son at the door of an overcrowded, understaffed orphanage.

When his ear became infected, as babies' ears will, the staff doctor prescribed medication. But it didn't seem to help; the baby just got sicker. The overworked staff had no time to give him extra care. His decline continued until the sister who headed the institution placed him in a box on her desk. She talked to him as she worked, going over the accounts with him in a gently crooning voice. She reached out to stroke him whenever she had a free hand. Under her loving attention, he began at last to thrive, until he was well enough to head across the Pacific to his new home.

Love is powerful medicine at any age: Vince can tell you that. Like Joseph, Vince is a foster father. Many years ago, he and Bianca took in a troubled twelve-year-old girl. Her father was an abusive alcoholic who made life torture for the child and her mother. One day she came home from school to find that her mother had found a way out of her misery: Her body was hanging in the basement.

Needless to say, this girl was a deeply troubled youngster when she came to live with Vince and Bianca. She was a failing student, prone to terrifying nightmares and temper tantrums. Winning her trust took a long time. Finally, her defenses yielded to their affection and she began to blossom. Her grades improved every year through high school. When she made the dean's list in college, Vince and Bianca were elated. Today her children call them Grandma and Grandpa, even though they were never able to adopt her legally.

Nurturing Life

These are dramatic cases. But even those of us who come to parenthood more easily soon discover that giving birth is only the beginning of the lengthy process of nurturing life in a child, just as loving a spouse into life is a lifelong venture. The rest is a matter of sleepless nights and tightened budgets, of joy and fear, of patient and unshakable love. God's call to give life necessarily involves making a commitment to nurture it.

For this reason, people who adopt a child earn the title "parent" as truly as those who welcome an infant conceived in their marriage bed. When Julia's adopted daughter, caught in the maelstrom of adolescent emotions, screamed that her "real mother" wouldn't treat her so badly, Julia was cut to the quick. "I am your real mom," she protested. "I didn't give birth to you, but I am still your forever mom."

As an adult, Julia's daughter made a successful search for her birth mother. Today they maintain a good relationship, but the younger woman, with the wisdom gained from her own experience of motherhood, calls the other by her first name, not "Mom."

The God who made us not only gives life but also continues to nurture it. That truth echoes through the Old Testament prophets. They depicted God as Israel's tender spouse and loving parent:

> *For as a young man marries a young woman,*
> *so shall your builder marry you,*
> *and as the bridegroom rejoices over the bride,*
> *so shall your God rejoice over you.* (Isaiah 62:5)

> *I led them with cords of human kindness,*
> *with bands of love.*
> *I was to them like those*
> *who lift infants to their cheeks.*
> *I bent down to them and fed them.* (Hosea 11:4)

And, of course, there came a day when God came into the world clothed in human flesh. Jesus of Nazareth himself stated his purpose for coming to earth: to bring life in abundance (see John 10:10). Through him, the fullness of life has come within our reach. Someday, we hold in faith, we will become all we were created to be and live forever in the presence of God.

But becoming all we were created to be begins in this life. We are called to become all God intended us to be. And that entails using our gifts well, following our inmost aspirations. Happily, those of us who marry don't have to find our way alone. For that call is part of the call that echoes through our marriages, as Hank long ago discovered.

"Judy and I began dating when we were in college,"

he remembers. "I was a music major because music was my first and only love. But I was only a fair instrumentalist. As a performer, I could have barely scraped out a living. My parents were urging me to consider teaching. That wasn't at all surprising to me; they were both educators. But I just couldn't see myself following in their footsteps."

"He was telling me this over pizza one night, and I understood perfectly. Teaching is the last thing I'd ever want to do." Judy's eyes begin to twinkle. "But when I went to tell him that, it didn't come out quite the way I intended. I just blurted out, 'I'd consider prostitution first!'"

"I think that was the moment when I really got serious about Judy," Hank says. "Those were the most liberating words I'd ever heard. I started talking to my adviser about other options, and ended up a music librarian. It's been a good life for me."

Hank's parents didn't want to force their son into a career he lacked enthusiasm for. They just wanted him to use his gifts wisely and well. We all want the best for the people we love. It's just not always clear to us how to make that happen, especially with our children. Even with each other, spouses sometimes question whether accepting a transfer to another city is worth the adjustment, or whether making a career move in a wholly different direction will work out well. But no good thing comes without a price tag. And love is always a risky investment.

Paying the Price

Giving life and investing care in another carries a steep price tag: vulnerability. On our wedding day, we promise to love each other until death parts us without recognizing the awful truth embedded in the fine print.

Mary Lou was in her fifties when her coworkers noticed that she seemed to be walking without quite touching the ground. She admitted that, after 15 years of widowhood, she had met a widower who delighted her. Soon she announced wedding plans. But for all her joy, there was a sober edge to her tone. "It's a lot harder," she said, "to say 'until death do us part' when you both know just what that means."

Having children escalates the vulnerability. "When we brought our first baby home," Amy states, "I expected to lose a lot of sleep, but I didn't have any idea how much I'd worry. When I said as much to my mom, she just laughed. 'Get used to it,' she told me. I'm still learning how right she was!" And worry we parents do—all our offspring's lives!

I remember cradling my own newborn daughter and watching the evening news. The headline story was the discovery of a little girl's body, raped and brutally murdered. I held my little one tighter and listened to a mother tiger I never knew existed roar inside me.

I still think of that moment whenever some football fan holds up a sign that says "John 3:16." That text reads, "For God so loved the world that he gave his only Son." I remember what happened to that Son on Calvary. I can imagine giving my own life for the sake of Jack or my kids, but my imagination will not stretch to offering them up for anyone. What an awesome thing it is to say that God willingly did something that would inflict so much pain on any human!

Relearning 'We'

For the *world* God gave the Son—not just for the Chosen People or for Jesus' contemporaries but for the whole human family. The God whose love knows no boundaries calls us ever to widen our circle of love.

Our intimate world began to widen even before we said, "I do," when we underwent the dreaded ordeal of meeting a sweetheart's family. Over the years since we welcomed those folks into our circle of kinship, we have forged bonds with them. Sometimes that was easy; in other cases, it took (and maybe still takes) great effort.

The extended family is not like it was just a few generations ago. I grew up in a house whose permanent residents included not only my parents and their kids but also my grandparents and an unmarried aunt. Another aunt lived with us while her husband served in the Second World War. Nowadays, many miles often separate family members; some of my own children and grandchildren live in distant states. Rarely do two generations share a home.

Yet telephones and modems keep families in close and life-giving touch. The wires hum with news of any crisis or happy event as we turn to one another for support. This intimate community helps us give life to our children, as well, for we cannot be doting grandparents to them. Neither can we provide the more objective view of an aunt or uncle or the sheer fun of being cousins.

We also pool our friends into a small community from whom we draw life and to whom we give life. My husband and I celebrated the dawn of the new century with the same friends we have been hugging at midnight for more than three decades. Together we have discovered who we are and what we value; together we have wrestled with faith and the vicissitudes of parenting, with suffering and with death.

And along the way, we discovered that, like the Trinity, the love we have shared as couples and as friends long ago began to open our arms ever farther. Our circle of friendship and kinship now also embraces the needy people whom Jesus called his least brothers and sisters (see Matthew 25:31-40). Each Christmas we celebrate our friendship with a gift to a local soup kitchen. In our immediate family, we exchange donations to charities of our choice. From the generosity of family and friends, we have learned to extend our care in many ways to the small planet that is our common home.

Sharing the Joy

Even as married folks, we came to know the price even God must pay to give life; we also came to know its joys. Giving life to each other in our lovemaking brought us a sense of awe at our own bodies. We sang with the psalmist, "I praise you, for I am fearfully, wonderfully made!" (Psalm 139:14). Welcoming infants into our hearts and our homes left us gasping with wonder. Perhaps no other event brings us such a keen sense of being very near to God, of becoming cocreators.

So do the moments when everything goes well with

our kids. Jenny remembers taking her four small children into a gift shop. "The sales clerk was noticeably nervous," she recalls. "But my kids had to go where I went or I'd never get out of the house. If I hadn't insisted that they look with their eyes, not their fingers, it would have been utter chaos. (My son thanked me for that lesson when he had his first job stocking shelves in a toy store. He couldn't believe how some people let their kids dismantle his work!)

"I went back to the same store a couple of months later—this time on a weekend when my husband stayed with the kids. The same salesperson said to me, 'I remember you. You're the one with the well-behaved children.' The Congressional Medal of Honor couldn't have made me prouder!"

The pleasure of having grown-up offspring caught Jack and me by surprise. One day we looked at them and realized that they had turned not only into capable adults but also into nice people whose company we enjoy. Most amazing of all, even the two who fought over every square inch of the room they shared are now good friends!

Grandchildren are, of course, a great delight. A friend says that's why they call them *grand*children, but I suspect the answer is even simpler. Grandparents don't have the day-in, day-out worries over budgets and grades and discipline and how these little people will turn out. Our job description is just one word long: Enjoy!

That brings us back to the definition of love that begins with the willingness to take delight in another. And it takes us back to the beginning of the Book of

Genesis, where God looked over the new-formed world and its abundance of life. God pronounced it good, very good and "rested"—leaned back and relaxed, I'm sure, with the biggest grin in history.

LOOKING BACK AT YOUR JOURNEY

- *In what ways has your spouse given life to you? How have you given life to him or her?*

- *If you have children, how did you feel the first time you held them in your arms? List the ways in which you have continued to give them life over the years.*

- *To whom outside your immediate family do you give life? How?*

- *Who outside your immediate family is life-giving to you? How?*

- *What costs to you has giving life in all those ways entailed?*

- *Consider the joy you have taken in the people you have loved into life. How does that help you realize what joy God takes in you?*

- *How has giving life led you to the Source of Life?*

CHAPTER FOUR

Achieving Reconciliation

OUR CALL FROM A FORGIVING GOD

*Jesus straightened up and said to her, "Woman, where are they? Has no one condemned you?" She said, "No one, sir." And Jesus said, "Neither do I condemn you. Go your way, and from now on do not sin again." —*John 8:10-11

Scripture gives her no name; she is just a woman wrenched from her lover's arms and dragged to the public square to be stoned to death for adultery. Jesus literally saves her life by inviting the person without sin to throw the first rock. And then he sends her on her way to make a fresh start, leaving us with tantalizing questions. What did she say to her husband when she got home? What did he say to her? Was he in the crowd at the marketplace, grasping a stone in an angry hand? Did Jesus' challenge move him to open his arms and his heart to her?

The questions haunt us because we know how essential forgiveness is to the survival of our own marriages. In a thousand small ways, it has become a daily habit. And yet forgiveness is no easier to define than love. We spend a lifetime learning just what it means to forgive, and in the process, we learn something more about God.

Forgiving Every Day

No two people living in such close proximity can avoid stepping on each other's toes from time to time. Every moment of carelessness, every lapse in thoughtfulness inflicts at least a scratch.

Jack has a habit of leaving drawers slightly open— an admittedly small thing that bugs me enormously. If I say anything, he bridles. So mostly I just follow him around and close them. Depending on my mood, I may close them hard. But after all these years, I doubt if he's suddenly going to notice that a drawer isn't shut tight, so all I can do is forgive the annoyance. It's not worth a divorce, and I doubt if I could plead spousal abuse to a murder charge.

Anyway, Jack would be the first to agree that I'm not perfect, either. He snores; I groan and mutter in my sleep. He takes forever to paint a wall; I rush and spatter paint everywhere. He loves to travel; I hate the very thought of packing. We have done our best to drive each other nuts over the years. It's a good thing we both have a sense of humor, for part of forgiving just goes back to that old definition of love: being willing to affirm the other's value and to take delight in him or her.

There's another factor in the need for constant forgiveness. When husband and wife come together at the end of a day that has been filled with frustration of some sort for either or both of them, whom do they take it out on? Who *can* they take it out on except each other? We are all hardest on the people who love us best. The rest of the world won't stand for our irritability. Another major factor in forgiving is putting ourselves in the other's shoes and making allowances for the pressures he or she is under.

People handle their grievances in different ways, as well. "I have often heard my next-door neighbors screaming at each other." Lisa shakes her head. "I'm glad we just retire to our corners and sulk when we're mad at each other. By the time we're ready to meet again, we have usually decided that whatever happened wasn't really worth much of a fuss." (Her neighbors, on the other hand, might insist that a good blowup clears the air.)

It's harder when a couple's styles are at variance. My grandmother used to rail at Grandpa at great length. (She would defend him just as fervently if anyone else attacked him.) She practiced what some marriage counselors call "gunnysacking": She saved up everything he had ever done wrong and dumped it all into each scolding. I remember walking out the door with him one time when Gram had been letting him have it. He touched his hearing aid and said, "There, now I can hear you." In response to my puzzled look, he explained, "I always shut it off when she starts jawing at me."

Most of us learn—albeit slowly—that what the marriage counselors say about gunnysacking is true: It is destructive. Raking up every old grievance just reopens old wounds. Our marriages survive because we break the habit. We discover that we resolve our differences most readily when we limit an argument to the issue at hand. And the Scriptures we hear in church point out to us that God doesn't gunnysack. When we resolve a spat with our Maker, the slate is wiped clean. As the prophet Isaiah says in God's words:

> Come now, let us argue it out,
>   says the LORD;
> though your sins are like scarlet,
>   they shall be like snow;
> though they are red like crimson,
>   they shall become like wool. (Isaiah 1:18)

"Forgive and forget" the old saw urges us. Yet forgetting is the least important part of forgiving. We may well remember an injury, but we focus harder on what is really important: why we love the person with whom we share a life. For it is that love that enables us to be patient with a spouse's shortcomings. Saint Paul begins his famous hymn to love (1 Corinthians 13:8-13), which we have heard at countless weddings, with that truth: "Love is patient."

Most of the things we forgive on a daily basis are not, after all, deliberate efforts to inflict injury. Rather, they rise out of the very differences that both draw us together and drive us mad. Too easily we forget that strength and weakness are the two sides of the same personality traits. It's all a matter of perception. We call the same characteristics by different names, depending on how we interpret them at any moment. The stubbornness that annoys us is also the perseverance we admire. The reticence that drives an extroverted partner crazy sometimes provides restful quiet. A partner's frugality is downright miserliness when the other's mood is extravagant. We often see fault in a virtue when the timing of its exercise is bad.

Jack, for instance, moves in one gear: low. Is his slowness an annoying fault or just one more sign of the steadiness I rely on so heavily? Depends on when you ask me! In my better moments, I'm willing to be patient.

Patience has always been God's strong suit, too, if we take the Scriptures seriously. Again and again the Old Testament describes God as "slow to anger and abounding in steadfast love" (see, for example, Exodus 34:6, Numbers 14:18, Psalms 86:15 and 103:8, Joel 2:3).

And when, at the end of a quarrel, I ask Jack if he still loves me, I think of Peter, my favorite biblical bungler. Immediately after naming him the first pope, Jesus predicted his own suffering and death. Peter, appalled by the thought, tried to dissuade Jesus—only to hear the Lord call him Satan and tell him to get lost (see Matthew 16:21-23). Peter couldn't handle it any better when Good Friday rolled around. Three times he denied knowing Jesus. After the Resurrection, Jesus simply asked Peter as many times for reassurance of his love (see John 21:15-17).

A Recurring Need

As if it weren't hard enough to deal with the irritations we're used to, life keeps pulling the rug out from under us. Some crises are predictable. Such things as the birth of child, a move, a job change, the emptying of the nest, retirement inevitably create new tensions in a couple's life together.

Patti remembers the birth of their first child as such a crisis. "We had tried so hard to get pregnant. We had to put up with all the indignities of fertility testing. And finally there was a baby on the way. We were ecstatic! But I wasn't prepared for what pregnancy did to my emotional balance. I cried all one evening because Ted didn't clear the dishes from the table. Can you imagine?

"When the baby came, she was the most beautiful creature we'd ever seen. She was also the crankiest. We were both dragging from lack of sleep—and getting as cranky as she was. For a while, we wondered if we were cut out for parenthood after all. Forget making love— she was sure to wake up and start fussing the minute we began.

"The baby, of course, outgrew her newborn fussiness, and we became lovers again. But the first few months were a real strain."

Bill's retirement was a tough time for Ellen. "I was working long hours as head nurse in the cardiac intensive care unit," she remembers. "We were just beginning to do heart transplants, and I was under a lot of pressure. I got way behind in things at home. The laundry piled up.

"One day Bill ran out of underwear. He could have called one of our grown-up kids for advice. He could have read the manuals on the shelf in the laundry room. He could even have read the instructions inside the washer lid. Instead, he solved the problem by eliminating it: He went out and bought more underwear. I could have killed him! That seemed a pretty messy solution, so I decided instead to clear up the mysteries of doing the wash for him."

Other crises sneak up on us without warning. Sharon, for example, didn't expect her thyroid gland to give out. For a while, she didn't even know it had. "All I knew was that I was terribly tired—and when I'm tired, I'm cross. I blamed it on the extra weight I was suddenly putting on. My doctor discovered an enlarged thyroid gland during a regular checkup and started me on replacement hormones. When I began to feel better, I realized that I had been more than just tired. I was totally apathetic; I couldn't work up any enthusiasm for anything."

"I didn't know what had happened to the girl I married," her husband adds. "Overnight she disappeared, leaving a stranger in her place."

Whether our differences rise from everyday tensions or from a sudden shift in life's direction, it is not always easy to forgive each other. Yet the truth we discovered when we were newly in love still holds: Making up is a joy.

I recently stood in the supermarket express lane behind a young man who was buying a lovely flower arrangement. I admired it and noted that it surely should get him some points. "I hope so," he replied with a smile. "I'm in the doghouse."

We usually express our reconciliation with some tangible sign. It may be flowers or homemade cookies or a bottle of wine. Most often it is a hug. But the very urge to celebrate the end of a quarrel expresses our instinctive conviction that a mended relationship is stronger than one that has never been tested.

When Forgiving Is Hard

The everyday need for forgiveness seems a far cry from the questions posed by the story of the woman taken in adultery. But some married couples have to find a way to forgive more serious injuries.

Jerry and Sue were one such couple. Maybe it was a midlife crisis that caused him to begin an affair with a coworker. Maybe it was just old-fashioned sinfulness. In any case, he ended up moving in with her.

Sue set out to punish him. And, like any long-married person who knows a spouse well, she knew exactly where to put the knife. Her skill in managing the budget had always been what he considered her best contribution to their partnership. So she threw frugality out the window. Armed with their credit cards, she went on a spending spree—and sent the bills to him.

I sometimes think that couples who are heading toward divorce put a lot of energy into stomping out the last embers of their love. That's certainly what Jerry and Sue were doing, until a pair of old friends, another married couple, stepped in.

"This is what you've worked for all these years?" the husband asked Jerry. "To live in this tiny apartment with this pretty young airhead?"

"What are you doing to yourself?" his wife asked Sue. "You have always prided yourself on being so practical. How well will all this stuff you're buying take Jerry's place?"

Slowly they came to their senses. And slowly they managed to forgive each other and start over again. When they celebrated their golden wedding anniversary, they offered a special toast to the couple "who have seen us through so much." Only a few of the guests knew what they meant.

What Sue's friend had helped her see was that forgiving is not something we do for the other person but something we do for our own sakes. "Wanting revenge so badly changed who I am," Sue admits. "I finally realized that it was making me into someone else, someone very different than the all-forgiving God who made me ever intended for me. It took time and effort for me to learn to trust Jerry again, but it was worth it. For too long I couldn't believe we'd see our golden anniversary."

It was Demon Rum, not an affair, that nearly broke up another marriage. When Phil's new job took him on the road regularly, Laura had trouble sleeping. "I'd be all over the bed looking for him," she explains. "I started getting up and having a drink to help me go back to sleep. Then I decided it would be better to have a drink before I went to bed. Or maybe a little bit before that, so I'd have time for a second and sleep really well."

"Then one day I finished my business a day earlier than I expected," Phil continues. "I caught an early flight and walked in our house to find her stumbling drunk. With a lot of help from a lot of people, I convinced her to enter a treatment program. But for months after she came out, I was a wreck every time I had to travel."

Laura chimes in: "He acted so suspicious, and I was working so hard to stay sober. Finally I asked him if he wanted a divorce, if he had stopped loving me. 'Honey,' he told me, 'I love you so much I can't stand it. Why do you think I urged you to get help? I just hated your drinking.' I remembered the old saying that God hates sin but loves sinners, and I felt like God had just hugged me."

Laura puts her finger on another essential aspect of forgiveness: separating the offense from the offender. Over the course of a lifetime, we do, to be sure, become the sum of our actions. We become thoughtful, loving people bit by bit, or we become hard and hateful one decision at a time. But we are, until the moment of our deaths, still works in progress. Whatever bad choices we may make, we are still capable of changing our course as long as we breathe—and as long as someone believes in that possibility as firmly as God does.

Learning to Trust Again

I don't know how couples manage to forgive really serious injuries. Happily, that's something I've never had to do. But I suspect it begins with the daily habit of letting the past become history and moving beyond it.

Tom found the way in an Easter season homily. Joann had left him for another man months before. Now she had thought better of it and was asking him to let her come home. Tom wasn't sure he could make that leap.

The Gospel that Sunday was John's account of Jesus' first appearance to his disciples in the upper room. He breathed the Holy Spirit into them and said, "If you forgive the sins of any, they are forgiven; if you retain the sins of any, they are retained" (John 20:23).

The Church has traditionally held this text as the foundation of the Sacrament of Penance, the homilist pointed out. But he went on to suggest that it applies not just to the clergy but also to all of us. "When we forgive someone," he explained, "we put the past behind us and find the freedom to move on. The person we forgive gains the same freedom.

"But when we don't forgive, we hold the moment of injury forever in the present. Both of us are forever trapped in that moment, unable to move ahead."

"His words rang true," Tom recalls. "I was stuck in the hurt, constantly reliving it. I couldn't see Joann as anything but a person who had done something terrible to me. I still couldn't see how we could manage a fresh start, but I decided to give it a try."

Discovering the Forgiving God

Perhaps it is when forgiving gets hardest that we come closest to God. Many centuries ago, the prophet Hosea told about his own experience with a faithless wife. Gomer didn't just have a brief fling; she played the harlot. But poor Hosea still loved her. He compared his situation to that of another anguished husband, faithless Israel's divine Lover.

And how did God resolve the issue? Hosea knew God as a jealous lover. The Ten Commandments were written in his heart: "[Y]ou shall worship no other god, because the LORD, whose name is Jealous, is a jealous God" (Exodus 34:14). Yet hear the words the prophet spoke on God's behalf:

> *Therefore, I will now allure her,*
> *and bring her into the wilderness,*
> *and speak tenderly to her....*
> *There she shall respond as in the days of*
> *her youth....*

> *And I will take you for my wife forever; I will*
> *take you for my wife in righteousness and in*
> *justice, in steadfast love, and in mercy. I will*
> *take you for my wife in faithfulness; and you*
> *shall know the LORD.* (Hosea 2:14, 15b, 19-
> 20)

Forever is a long time indeed, much longer than the
lifetime husbands and wives have pledged to each other.
It is, I suppose, inevitable that the God whose very
nature is love can promise everlasting mercy and
fidelity. The rest of us must limp along as best we can,
day by day offering forgiveness and a fresh start to each
other.

LOOKING BACK AT YOUR JOURNEY

- *How do you deal with anger or disappointment? Does your*
  style match your spouse's? If not, what is the difference?

- *How do you and your spouse usually resolve your*
  differences?

- *What do you have to forgive your spouse for most often?*
  For what does your spouse frequently have to forgive you?

- *Which of your spouse's traits do you sometimes see as faults*
  and other times as virtues?

- *What have you learned about the difference between*
  forgiving and forgetting?

- *When have you and your spouse been held fast in a bad*
  moment because one of you refused to forgive the other?
  How did you break free?

- *How would you define forgiveness?*

- *How has your experience of forgiving and being forgiven led you to the all-forgiving God?*

CHAPTER FIVE

Facing Sorrow

OUR CALL FROM A COMPASSIONATE GOD

They were all weeping and wailing for her; but [Jesus] said, "Do not weep; for she is not dead but sleeping." ...[H]e took her by the hand and called out, "Child, get up!" Her spirit returned, and she got up at once. Then he directed [her parents] to give her something to eat. — LUKE 8:52, 54-55

Jairus and his wife were pious, God-fearing people. Every week she lit the candles to herald the approach of Sabbath. He led prayer in the local synagogue, where Jesus had been teaching and healing. When their only daughter fell seriously ill, Jairus hurried to Jesus and begged him to come and cure her. But Jesus was delayed by another's needs, and by the time he arrived, the child was dead.

No, not dead, but only sleeping, Jesus told them. Someone snickered at his ignorance, and soon the house resounded with jeering laughter. But Jesus took the child's hand and told her to get up—and she did! Their tears transformed by joy, Jairus and his wife embraced the little girl and turned to thank Jesus. He smiled at their daughter and gently asked, "You're hungry, aren't you?" And her parents hurried to get her something to eat.

When the World Falls Apart

In good times and bad; in sickness and health: Those are the terms of our wedding-day promise to love each other all our lives. Rough times do come, and they are always worse than we dreamed in the starry-eyed bliss of the wedding day. Serious illness strikes; job loss threatens our security; death strikes close to home; fire or storm hits a house. Such events shatter the world we thought we knew and leave us buried in the wreckage. Some couples cling more tightly to each other in the rubble. Kate and Joe did. When Joe was scheduled for a business meeting in London, they totaled the frequent flyer miles and decided to turn it into a holiday for two. When they came back, she thought nothing of the ache in her calf. "We had, after all, spent a lot of hours cramped in tourist-class seats," she explains. "But a day or two later, I suddenly couldn't breathe."

It wasn't a tired muscle at all. It was a blood clot that had found its way into her lung. She spent a week in the hospital and came home with all the strength of overcooked pasta.

"Joe was wonderful," she remembers. "He waited on me hand and foot and told me how much he loved me more often than he did on our honeymoon."

Joe reaches for her hand. "I came close to losing her," he explains. "She is the best gift God ever gave me, and I just took her for granted. I'll never do that again!" (He probably has—don't we all?)

The stress of a crisis can just as easily put nearly unbearable strain on a relationship. When Harry lost his job in a company reorganization, Jo tried to be supportive. They sat down together and added up their resources, looking for places to trim the budget until he found another job. Together they decided that Harry would work regular hours at job hunting—get resumes out there, contact everyone he knew who might have a lead and so on.

But they didn't calculate on the loss of self-esteem that comes with a job loss. Harry became depressed. He'd sit for hours, just staring into space.

"He couldn't market himself well because he no longer had confidence in his own abilities," Jo remembers. "Meanwhile, I was trying to run the household on a shoestring. He'd blow his top over every unexpected expense—and unemployment sure didn't make them come any further apart. I retaliated by snapping at him all day long.

"It was nine long months before he found a new job. Only by the grace of God did our marriage survive that long."

Seeking God's Help

We believers depend on the grace of God to get us through a lot. Saint Paul came to believe that grace was all he needed when he cried out to God for relief. "Three times I appealed to the Lord about this,... but he said to me, 'My grace is sufficient for you, for power is made perfect in weakness'" (2 Corinthians 12:8-9).

When tragedy cripples us, leaving us weak even in faith, we have to search for new strength. When familiar habits of prayer fail us, we have to rethink our concepts of God and seek signs of divine love in places we may not have thought to look before.

We certainly don't settle into peace of mind as quickly as the great Apostle to the Gentiles. Like Jairus, we do our best to impress upon the Lord the urgency of our situations. We plead, we bargain, we cry out for reasons. But God remains silent. And one more certainty falls into the rubble that surrounds us: our faith in a loving God. We ask how we have fallen out of divine favor. We wonder if God has simply forgotten us.

Glimpses of God's Love

No, we are not forgotten. Many centuries ago, God made a promise in poignantly human terms:

> *Can a woman forget her nursing child,*
> *or show no compassion for the child of her womb?*
> *Even these may forget,*
> *yet I will not forget you.* (Isaiah 49:15)

In time, the God who spoke through the prophet took flesh in Jesus of Nazareth. In Jesus, God drew close enough to comfort people with a human voice, a human touch, a human smile. God still likes to work that way. Because of our relationship with Jesus, we ourselves are his body—his eyes, his voice, his comforting embrace. Jesus no longer walks through the streets of the world. Now he yearns to use the people who are his Body to continue bringing comfort in any need. Indeed, he even described the Last Judgment in those terms: "Come, you that are blessed by my Father, inherit the kingdom prepared for you from the foundation of the world; for I was hungry and you gave me food, I was thirsty and you gave me something to drink, I was a stranger and you welcomed me, I was naked and you gave me clothing, I was sick and you took care of me, I was in prison and you visited me" (Matthew 25:34-36).

Now we feel his touch through other members of his Body: the people who offer us their support in many ways. Jack and I once brushed against the horror of losing a child. Our second daughter was born ten weeks prematurely, weighing in at just over three pounds. In the early 1960's, such a tiny baby's hold on life was highly precarious. We clung to the loving presence of family and friends.

To be sure, no one knows exactly how another feels when tragedy strikes, for each of us is unique. But some people seem to have an instinct for sensing the pain others feel. And some speak to our sorrow from their own experience. The two people who gave us the most support when our baby's life hung in the balance were folks we didn't know very well—people who had been there themselves.

One was my sister's neighbor, whose preschooler's beginnings had been just as inauspicious. She wrote a letter that touched exactly what we were feeling—our hopes that the baby would not only make it but also would develop normally in spite of her rough start. (She did; now forty, she was an honor student all through school.)

The other was a neighbor who told the story of her grandmother's equally premature birth. She arrived in the dead of a bitter winter in a remote Ohio farmhouse. The country doctor who delivered her couldn't get her to start breathing. In desperation, he told the neighbor's wife who was helping him to fetch a teaspoonful of water with a couple of drops of whiskey in it. When he tipped it into the baby's mouth, she began to choke and sputter. The woman had gotten the proportions backward, but the burning jolt startled the little one into life.

There were no incubators or oxygen tanks in those days. For the next two months, the mother sat by the hot stove with the tiny bundle on her lap, rocking her day and night while her husband waited on them with great care. That baby was in her eighties when our little girl was born.

The comfort we experience doesn't necessarily depend on what someone finds to say, according to Maria. When she and her husband brought his mother home to nurse her through a long recovery from surgery, friends and neighbors pitched in. They brought meals, ran errands, took the laundry home and cut the grass—a thousand helpful gestures of concern.

"One day a woman whose face I knew from church but had never actually met showed up at our door with a casserole," she relates. "When I told John, he burst into tears. I had cried a lot, but he is a stiff-upper-lip guy. It was joy and gratitude that got to him. 'With so much love around us,' he told me, 'how can anything really hurt us?'"

Reaching Out

If our own pain makes us more sensitive to other people's hurt, the care we receive also teaches us the importance of trying to bring comfort.

The Gospels portray Jesus as one of those people whose antennae are always set to pick up someone's deepest sorrow. And when we count the people who have been where we are, we must include him. He never suffered from corporate downsizing or nursed his own child through a dangerous illness or buried a wife. But in Jesus, God knew what it is like to be human from the inside. Jesus learned what gladdens our hearts: laughter shared with beloved friends, the warmth of sunshine on our shoulders, the taste of a meal enriched by good company.

He also knew what it was like to be misunderstood by the closest people, the way those in power resist new ideas, the agony of betrayal by someone who should have been trustworthy. He wept in grief at the tomb of his good friend Lazarus. And, of course, he came to know the whip and the slow suffocation of the cross, the jeers of a hate-filled crowd and desertion by the people he counted on the most.

It is to the cross that believers' eyes turn when life goes horribly wrong. And it is the cross that draws us out of ourselves when we discover that someone else is in pain—especially if we have known the same pain ourselves. For we remember that he invited us to pick up the cross and follow him.

We often interpret that invitation as an insistence that we are to bear whatever sorrows come our way with patience and faith in God's will. Some people speak of God's will only when tragedy strikes. That hardly seems fair to me, unless we are equally quick to speak of God's will when life is sweet!

Yet it is true that the sorrows we experience teach us compassion. In that sense, we can truly speak of God's will, for they fine-tune the divine likeness in us. From them we learn the value of making small gestures, of imitating Jesus' concern not only for a little girl's life but also for her appetite.

Our anxiety over a very wee baby returned in force when dear friends' baby died suddenly in his crib. Had I Jesus' power to restore life to a dead child, I'd certainly have done so. But there seemed nothing I could do to ease their unthinkable loss. So when they asked me to serve as lector at the funeral, of course I said yes.

Nothing prepared me for the size of the casket the funeral director carried up the aisle. I was a pretty inexperienced lector; I don't know how I managed to stumble through the Scripture passage. But when I finished, the baby's dad smiled at me and mouthed, "Thank you."

Later I apologized to him for not having read as well as I wanted to. "It was beautiful," he protested. "It was beautiful because you were there for us."

Again I thought back to the tense days when our daughter was new, and I realized that what he said was true. It is not what we do that matters; our inability to perform miracles in no way diminishes the comfort we can bring. It was their child's healing that Jairus and his wife sought from Jesus. Once she was dead, they wanted only to take comfort from his presence—and powerful comfort such presence can always be. The most priceless gift we can give is simply the gift of being there.

Broadening Our Concern

We first offer that most precious of gifts to the people with whom we are most naturally drawn, to family and friends and neighbors. But it cannot end there, for suffering does not observe the familiar boundaries we draw around our love.

It was their son's appendectomy that stretched the horizons for Pam and Terry. "I got to talking with other couples in the waiting room," Terry remembers. "There was a young woman there whose child was undergoing cancer surgery—and not for the first time, either. Another couple's kid was getting another skin graft after being badly burned. It sounds silly, but I really felt guilty because our boy was just getting his appendix out."

"We talked about it later," Pam adds. "And we thought there must be something we could do to help other couples through their children's serious illnesses. We looked around for opportunities to help, and got involved with the local Ronald McDonald House, which provides a place for out-of-towners to stay while their kids are hospitalized in our city."

It wasn't a stranger that broke through the Connors's shell but people they knew all too well. They had long wished that the Schultzes lived anywhere in the world but next door to them. Relations between the two couples were tense from day one.

"We had every argument neighbors can have," they explain. "Their kids were impossible. They constantly wreaked havoc on our property. And the parents weren't any better—thoughtless, nosy, loud. They put up a fence and decided that a root from our tree was in the way. They took a hatchet to the root and seriously damaged the trunk, as well. After that, we just avoided them. We didn't even say hello when we saw them.

"And then they had a bad fire. She was hospitalized for smoke inhalation and was in pretty bad shape for a while. We couldn't help but feel bad about them. So we did what neighbors do: sent meals over, kept the kids while he went to visit her.

"The really strange thing is that we discovered they weren't such awful people after all."

Jesus preached love even for enemies. "You have heard that it was said, 'You shall love your neighbor and hate your enemy.' But I say to you, love your enemies and pray for those who persecute you, so that you may be children of your Father in heaven; for he makes his sun rise on the evil and on the good, and sends rain on the righteous and on the unrighteous" (Matthew 5:43-45).

His words were not altogether startling news to the people who listened to them the very first time. Every spring, they celebrated the Passover, remembering that their history began when God's great saving act delivered their ancestors from slavery in Egypt. Every year, they recalled the story of the tenth plague God visited on the Egyptians, the death of a whole people's firstborn children, and how they were spared because they marked their doorposts with the blood of a sacrificed lamb.

And during the meal, they spilled out ten drops

from the ritual cup of wine in solemn tribute to the Egyptians' suffering—as their descendants still do today. That act continues to acknowledge the hard truth that enemies are God's children, too.

Without a Word

As a wise preacher once pointed out, the opposite of love is not hatred but apathy. Our journey together has taught us the importance of people who care. Slowly over the years, we have learned that being willing to stand with someone who is hurting, however helpless we feel, expresses love more powerfully that anything else we can do. People who are willing just to be with us in our sorrow give us new insight into what God is like. And sometimes they don't have to say anything, as Nan discovered.

Her husband was seriously injured in an automobile accident. During the weeks he spent in intensive care, a friend came to sit with her at least for a little while every day. "She didn't say much," Nan reports. "She just sat there with me. It made me think of all the times Ken and I have spoken volumes about our love without saying a word. I began to wonder if God's silence isn't like that. Now, instead of straining to hear an answer to my prayers, I think of her. And I try just to relax in the arms that are holding me."

LOOKING BACK AT YOUR JOURNEY

- *What sorrows have you had to face as a couple?*

- *Who and what gave you comfort? How?*

- *What insight has your suffering given you into other people's pain? How have you responded to the sorrows of others?*

- *How far from the intimate circle of family and friends has your concern stretched?*

- *Was there ever a time when you were moved by the suffering of an enemy? What did you do?*

- *What loving silences have you known with your spouse? With others?*

- *How has your experience of loving silence helped you understand God's silence when you cry out in pain?*

- *How has your experience of suffering led you to the compassionate God?*

CHAPTER SIX

Letting Go

OUR CALL FROM AN OPEN-HANDED GOD

As [Jesus] went a little farther, he saw James son of Zebedee and his brother John, who were in their boat mending the nets. Immediately he called them; and they left their father Zebedee in the boat with the hired men, and followed him.—MARK 1:19-20

Zebedee surely overheard Jesus' conversation with his sons from the other side of the small boat from which they fished together. Whatever it was about, this stranger who so completely won John and James must have impressed their father, too, for he made no move to stop them. Still, he must not have found it easy to watch the boys go off with Jesus, leaving him to carry on the family business alone.

Worse yet, he had to go home and explain to his wife why their sons weren't coming home for supper. It is not hard to imagine Mrs. Z.'s reaction. "They went where? With whom? And you just let them go? Didn't you think I'd like to say good-bye? We may never see them again!"

Maybe he explained how his heart had leaped with the hope that this was the long-awaited Messiah and that his boys were headed for greatness in his court. If so, Zebedee was certainly persuasive, for we later find Mrs. Z. asking Jesus to grant James and John seats of honor beside his throne (see Matthew 20:20-23).

Scripture, of course, doesn't record the couple's conversation. The only time we meet Zebedee is when his sons leave him at the water's edge. But Mrs. Z. appears one more time in the Gospel. She is among the women who stand beneath the cross on Good Friday, watching Jesus die—and with him all her dreams of glory for her sons (see Matthew 27:55-56).

Loosening Our Grip

Knowing how the story of Zebedee's sons ends blunts for us the impact of the losses he and his wife faced. Their sons, partners in the family fishing business, left home, taking with them their parents' dreams of a secure old age. (Social Security and pension plans were many centuries away.) In an era when small distances loomed large, Mr. and Mrs. Z. couldn't expect regular phone calls, E-mail or even snail mail.

Their hopes for their sons' success as Jesus' lieutenants were dashed first by Jesus himself and then by the Messiah's apparently total defeat. They had to let go of their most cherished dreams and of the people who embodied them.

To have and to hold: That was our wedding day dream. But we quickly found that before we could hold we had to let go. We each went to the altar with a model of marriage we had absorbed from watching our parents together. Their unions were the models we expected (whether consciously or unconsciously) to imitate—or, perhaps, the disasters we were determined to avoid.

But we quickly discovered that our spouses' parents were not the same as our own. Nita explains: "My family is physically affectionate. My parents are always hugging and kissing each other and us. But my father-in-law is really inhibited about displays of affection. He absolutely stiffens when I put my arms around him.

"I was shocked to discover that my husband is just like him. It's not that he's cold—far from it! I couldn't ask for a better lover. But he considers any caress solely as a prelude to lovemaking. He doesn't ever want just to sit and hold my hand or let me put my head on his shoulder while we watch TV. When he leaves on a business trip, I'm lucky to get a good-bye peck. He wouldn't think to volunteer a hug."

Many of us discovered early on that we were individuals with different, even discordant needs. When Gabe and Martha married, they already knew their personalities were very different and they liked their complementarity. He was an outgoing salesman; she a quiet accountant. But they soon discovered that very different expectations rose from their personalities.

As Gabe tells it, "I'd come home from work wanting to talk about my day—about the people I had dealt with, about the successes and about the things that hadn't gone so well. But Martha didn't seem terribly interested at first; later she got downright short with me. Who wouldn't feel rejected?"

Martha puts another spin on the problem. "My job

requires dealing with people all day long. When I get home, I'm exhausted. I want nothing more than to be alone for a while, to regroup, as it were. Quiet time restores my strength."

Letting the person we love best be who he or she is goes beyond learning to celebrate our differences. It can be a wrenching act of letting go—letting go of who we think she is, of what we think he ought to be. And in the effort, we begin to sense what it means to say that God loves us just as we are.

A Question of Ownership

I am reluctant to sing hymns that insist we exist under divine ownership because God loves us. All the world and everything in it—including us—belong to God. We are *free* because the God who loves us made us that way. The notion that loving someone makes that person mine contradicts everything I have learned of love. I belong to Jack because I love him. We belong to our grown children because we long ago surrendered our hearts to them, but they are ours only because they freely hold us in affection in spite of the way we fumbled through parenthood. Possessive love only stifles and alienates the objects of our affections.

Someone once observed that some things cannot be held tightly. A butterfly may light on your extended finger, but if you try to clasp it, you either frighten it away or crush it. You can gather running water in cupped hands, but you cannot close your fingers around it; it will simply run through them. Just so, we can only hold the people we love with open hands.

That becomes especially apparent when we welcome children into our lives. They too, of course, elude our ideas of who they are; the personality traits with which they come are not of our choosing. And one of the first things we teach them is to wave bye-bye. Sometimes we have to leave them for a while, raising their instinctive fear of abandonment. Waving good-bye provides a momentary distraction from their terror.

They learn to say good-bye all too well, for one day they will leave us. We know from the beginning that the goal of parenthood is to guide them toward independent adulthood, yet, in practice, many of the steps along the way are hard. The first ride down the street alone on a tricycle, the first day of school, the first driver's license: All these milestones can make a parent's heart heavy. And comes the day when they leave home to start life on their own, we have to let go of part of our own identities.

I always thought my friend Madge had it all together. She had a serious career as part of the administration of a large school district. While I was trying to figure out how to make it through the next week, she'd talk about her latest five-year plan.

But when the last of her boys left home for good, Madge had a nervous breakdown.

"I couldn't face the thought of not being their mom anymore," she explains. "Oh sure, I'm still their mother, but not in the same way. They don't need me to take care of them anymore. I was depressed because I was grieving for part of myself that was gone forever. It took me a long time to realize that an empty nest could be a fun place to live for the two of us. I certainly hadn't imagined that a whole new relationship with our sons was in store for us. We are still exploring the wonders of having our kids turn into adult friends."

Giving the Freedom to Fail

From time to time, the people we love make bad decisions. We soon learn to let our children take the consequences when the price is low. Louise's oldest daughter, for example, was a dreadful dawdler, "one of the folks my father-in-law always called 'the late Logans.' One day when she was in kindergarten, I tired of trying to hurry her and let her miss the bus—and the day. A day out of kindergarten is not a major loss in the great educational scheme, but she was so crushed she changed her pace. At least before school, she moved a little faster and never missed the bus again.

"In middle age, she is still one of the folks for whom God made the last minute, and I suspect she always will be, but she has never missed a plane."

We are reluctant to let our kids take more serious consequences. Marla struggled to cope with her teenager's decision to drop out of college after two quarters and get a job. "I was concerned, of course, about the long-range effect on his future," she remembers. "The only thing on his mind was trying his wings. He found a job that paid a little more than minimum wage, and moved in with a group of friends who were renting a house. What a pigpen that was!

"It seems like it took forever—it must have been nearly a year—before he decided that there must be more to life than a dead-end job. One day he came home with a brochure about nursing school, and the next thing we knew he was not only enrolled but loving it. He worked his tail off for his certificate, and went on to get his bachelor's degree in night school. Now he has a master's degree in anesthesia and a high-paying job that gives him joy.

"When he took honors in the master's program, I told him that we always knew he could do it. Know what he said? 'I think I always knew that, too. It just took me a long time to figure out that I *wanted* to do it!'"

Marla's son found a happy ending. But we know all too well that some kids don't. And, of course, we want to spare them the pain that comes from making disastrous choices.

Jesus called God *Abba,* an intimate term for "Father." "Look at the birds of the air," he said; "they neither sow nor reap nor gather into barns, and yet your heavenly Father feeds them. Are you not of more value than they?" (Matthew 6:26). Yet this loving parent takes a great risk with the children who are so precious. God doesn't restrain us when we head for disaster; rather, we are allowed to throw our lives away—even forever—if we so choose. God took an even greater risk in sending the beloved Son to show us how to live. That precious child died a shameful and painful death.

Such open-handedness may strike our understanding of parenthood as uncaring. Saint Paul, to whom control of his fractious children in faith was certainly an important issue, wrestled with his own people's refusal to accept Jesus. "I want you to understand this mystery: a hardening has come upon part of Israel...," he wrote to the Church in Rome. Still he insists that Israel will nevertheless yet be saved "for the gifts and calling of God are irrevocable" (Romans 25b, 29).

So is a parent's love. Our children may break our hearts, but we cannot retract the love we have invested in them. Just ask Bob. His son is on death row, and Bob is fighting to save his life. "I can't excuse what he did," he admits. "But taking his life won't undo the pain he has caused. And he's still our son. We love him and we want him to live." His face grows thoughtful. "I guess that's what God wants for all of us."

Indeed it is. God wants the same thing we want for our children. In the words of an ancient prophet: "For this is the way of which Moses, while he was still alive, spoke to the people, saying, 'Choose life for yourself, so that you may live!'" (2 Esdras 7:129).

God wishes more than mere survival for us. "I came that they may have life, and have it abundantly," Jesus said (John 10:10). Finally we realize that it is not just survival our open-handed God wishes for us, but the fullness of life willingly embraced. And the fullness of life is something we grow toward, slowly, over the course of a lifetime.

Growing Together

We watch our children grow, of course. But we also watch each other grow. Even as we count the graying or thinning of each other's hair, we also note more inward changes. Many of them can be directly attributed to living together, as we slowly blend our two disparate selves into one. For just as surely as we married someone who somehow completes us, who is the other half of ourselves, over the years we gradually internalize our other half.

"After 35 years," Paul explains, "I can complete Sal's sentences. That's a bit scary. What's even scarier is that I catch myself *thinking* like her!

"When we were young, we divided our concerns according to our strengths. I think pretty concretely, so I dealt with *things*. Earning a living, balancing the checkbook, fixing whatever needed to be fixed: That was my area. Sal, on the other hand, concerns herself with how people feel. She was always the one who knew when it was time to call or visit someone who was troubled, what would delight the birthday child, what to say at the funeral home.

"Funny, nowadays I'm just as quick as she is to pick up on how someone feels. At the office I'm known as the guy with the big shoulders, the one who can always sense when things aren't going right for a coworker. And Sal's developed a practical streak she never had when her hair was still black. Sometimes I wonder if we're turning into one another!"

But that's the whole idea, isn't it? That's exactly what Jesus was dreaming of when he prayed at the Last Supper: "Father, I ask not only on behalf of these [the disciples at table with him], but also on behalf of those who will believe in me through their word, that they may all be one. As you, Father, are in me and I am in you, may they also be in us…" (John 17:20-21).

With all believers, we are called to let go even of our very selves and become one with God. We learn how that works as we let go of our limited selves and make our spouses truly part of who we are. Our marriage is our training ground for heaven.

The Last Good-bye

Before we attain the fullness of life, however, we face one more act of letting go, one that is terribly wrenching. Sooner or later, the day anticipated in our wedding vows, the day death will separate us, draws near. One day, whether it comes upon us suddenly or over a long period, we must say a last good-bye to each other—to all the years we have shared, to all the dreams yet unfulfilled, to the other half of ourselves.

The parting is excruciatingly painful for the one who is left behind. It is no less painful for the one who goes first, for nothing is harder to let go of than life on this earth. As one dying friend put it, "You know what you have here, and it's hard to leave."

My dad didn't want to leave. Mortally ill, he refused to talk about his prospects for recovery, though he surely knew as well as the rest of us that he wasn't getting any better and wasn't likely to. One day my mother couldn't stand it any more. "Sandy," she said to him, "you never went anywhere without telling me good-bye."

A silent tear rolled down his cheek. Behind it came at last the flood of words he had been unable to release. Together he and Mother counted their memories, their reluctance to part, their hope of meeting again one day. A few days later, he died peacefully.

Marcia was much more ready to go, but her husband couldn't loosen his grip on her. Day after day, he sat beside her hospital bed, begging her not to leave him. One evening she sent him home early. "I'm tired, hon," she told him. "Go home now and let me get some sleep. You need some rest yourself." Within an hour of his departure, she slipped away. As Jesus surrendered his spirit into his Father's hands from the cross, she let go of life and fell into the loving arms that had held her all through her life.

Someday, one of us must go on alone. The death of a spouse leaves a monstrous hole in the heart. "At first, every day brought a new reminder that he wasn't there," Ruth remembers. "You're really busy for a while writing thank-you notes and taking care of business. But suddenly one day there's nothing left to do but what you've been avoiding: clean out his closet. And just when you thought that was the hardest part, the death certificate comes and your loss is new all over again.

"For months I'd wake up in the night and wonder why there was no one on the other side of the bed—and remember why. The calendar became my worst enemy. Every Tuesday became the Tuesday he died. Holidays, birthdays in the family, our anniversary—nightmares!

"I tried visiting the cemetery, but he wasn't there. I went back to the town we lived in until our retirement years, but he wasn't there, either. He was in heaven, I thought—but where is heaven?

"Finally I realized that where I could best find him was inside myself. Not just in my memories, although I fingered them like the beads on my rosary. No, where he really was is someplace deep in who I am. I don't know quite how to explain that. Somehow we became part of each other over the years. Part of me died with him, but part of him still lives in me. And one day we'll get our two parts back together again."

Ruth is right. For the God who has been calling us through all the twists and turns of married life waits for us at the journey's end. Then we will see that everything we have held in lovingly open hands is still ours, that every loss we have suffered has also been a gain.

LOOKING BACK AT YOUR JOURNEY

- *In what ways have you had to let go of each other through the years of your marriage? When was it hardest?*

- *When and how did letting go bring you closer?*

- *What dreams have you had to relinquish over the years? Which was the hardest to let go?*

- *If you have children, what have you learned about letting go in your relationship with them?*

- *Which period in your life together has required the most wrenching letting go of what had been? What did you gain in the process?*

- *Whom do you hold with open hands? How has doing that enriched your relationship with them?*

- *How has having to let go led you to the open-handed God?*

Holding On to the Dream

Then afterward
I will pour out my spirit on all flesh;
your sons and your daughters shall prophesy,
your old men shall dream dreams,
and your young men shall see visions.
                                        —JOEL 2:28

The dreams we hold today are very different from the ones that filled our eyes with stars on our wedding day. The years have seen some of those dreams come true; others we had to lay aside as unrealistic. And yet, at heart they are the same. We still yearn to spend the rest of our lives with the one person we cannot help but call our other half.

That dream first took form in God's heart before the world began. It first reached fruition when Eve joined Adam in the garden: "Therefore a man leaves his father and mother and clings to his wife, and they become one flesh" (Genesis 2:24). It is God who keeps whispering it in our ears, encouraging us to travel farther on the path that leads us home.

In these pages, we have looked back at that journey. It is not over yet; we still have, we hope, a long way to go. Only one thing is certain about the road ahead: It is strewn with the same old orange barrels.

May you continue to find your way through them and enjoy the rest of the journey!